and for Alfred,
with my best,

Debora

Princeton Series of Contemporary Poets

For Other Books in the Series
see page 81

and

poems by
Debora Greger

Princeton University Press

Library of Congress Cataloging in Publication Data will be found on the last
printed page of this book

ISBN 0-691-06646-9
ISBN 0-691-01423-X (Pbk.)

Publication of this book has been aided by a grant from the Paul Mellon Fund of
Princeton University Press

This book has been composed in Linotron Bodoni

Clothbound editions of Princeton University Press books are printed on acid-free
paper, and binding materials are chosen for strength and durability. Paperbacks,
although satisfactory for personal collections, are not usually suitable for library
rebinding

Printed in the United States of America by Princeton University Press,
Princeton, New Jersey

Acknowledgments

Agni Review: "The Garden of Acclimatization"

American Poetry Review: "Book of Hours," "Life Drawing," "Queen of a Small Country"

Black Warrior Review: "The Corner of Delicious and Jonathan Streets," "Laundry," "Natural History"

Epoch: "Of"

Georgia Review: "Graces"

Grand Street: "Pastorale"

Iowa Review: "The Shallows"

The Nation: "The Roman Baths at Chesters," "To Market," "To Speak of Water Music"

The New Republic: "Grounds," "Habit, Those Yards," "Long Island Real Estate: Great Neck"

The New Yorker: "Everyday Things," "Precipitation"

Poetry: "Dream Lecture, June," "Passage Overland," "Two Rodin Torsos"

Sewanee Review: "Second Movement: Adagio," "This Underwater Room Where You Swim, Scaled"

Southwest Review: "And," "There, There"

Yale Review: "Piranesi in L.A."

Special thanks to the Mary Ingraham Bunting Institute of Radcliffe College, the Ingram Merrill Foundation, and the Amy Lowell Poetry Traveling Scholarship

for James Merrill
and
for Anita Thacher

We often think that when we have completed our study of *one* we know all about *two* because "two" is "one and one." We forget that we still have to make a study of "and."

—SIR ARTHUR EDDINGTON

Contents

I

The Shallows

Rolling pants' legs, bundling skirts,
they have come down the shore with gunny sacks,

bird cages, dresses knotted together—
tonight not the moon but a run of smelt

silvers the shallows, night water's deep opacity.
Gray gone black, the wet sand chills, floor-hard

as long as, like those boys, I don't stand still.
Coaching and taunting, a chorus of spring frogs,

they leap the fish. Even the woman I've seen
walking daily in the village is here, the one

with her arm in a sling and a three-legged dog.
Her slowed passage rippling the crowd,

she's the domestic tamely obscured
by the raucous dark. Down from this inlet,

a basket of lights lists where the family living
on the grounded freighter finishes another

tilted day. Finally, I think, that canted home
would seem no longer maddening or novel

but cramped like any other. Out in its vast
and watery front yard, below the level of all this,

a cold current tunnels unremittingly north.

3

Everyday Things

Think of the swimming
that does for flight in dreams—feet
dragging through leaves, you watch

yourself climb through a stagy light,
like this afternoon's, doubly lit
by lamps and weaker sun. How can you

not believe the merely visible?
A boy struggles into costume
over a harness that's half the magic

of theatrical flying. Like humans,
ducks are slipping on the river,
feet out from under them

across the ice. Tossed from a window,
the carrier pigeon charts a course
as long as the night stays clear,

leaving me, armchaired, to imagine
a message worth wingbeats per mile
as ground traversed brings closer

nothing but dawn. The chair's
upholstered wings shelter, stiffly;
maybe the painter was right about

a floating world: chair not resting on
but hovering just above the floor,
everyday wings keeping us

from collisions that are touch
without will. I wanted to be a book—
pages riffling with pinions,

coverts, underwings, primary
and secondary feathers of flight,
its wings falling open in your hands.

Book of Hours

Economically, she gathers her hair in one hand,
and bends to drink at the fountain.
You can see down her shirt.

If this were the beginning of a story,
you'd think so she is that kind of woman—
a dancer in street dress who can't

cover practiced grace. You might
not be right, just a man who wants
to sleep with some idea or who's read

that Chekhov described a character in *The Seagull*
simply as wearing checked trousers.
As in the Limbourgs' miniature of October,

a gesture illumines or betrays. Everything
has a little shadow: plowman and beast,
scarecrow, magpies, man sowing,

and footprints of that man. At the river
boats are buoyed by their reflections;
a washerwoman's image bends back so accurately

it's an abstract of the momentary. Silhouette
in the solid light, you're a man like others,
observing a breast's disembodied curve

against cloth as if later the violence
of looking, like so many buttons,
can be romantically ripped undone.

Dream Lecture, June

Today we discuss what the thunder
said to Mr. Eliot. What do I mean
by "we" that doesn't include you?
Take condensation, the very air rising
to answer rhetorical questions
on loftier planes. So in his vault
under the street, through glass
embedded in the walk, a man could sense
the light go under, the rushed rain
of footsteps give way to a condescending
like footnotes, first syllables suggesting
common knowledge the rest pointedly deny.
Even as you mark off another minute,
eighteen hundred thunderstorms forego
polite discourse. "Close," we term such air.
A second, and a hundred lightning bolts
split charred sentences. This
is what we mean by "discuss," not
your family of arguments but
the clash of charged ions rumbling
as I tear my notes. You don't believe me.
Lightning's jags cut the easiest swath
to earth. But trace them back
up the whole sky I wave before you,
chambermaid in a sanatorium beating a rug,
or patient playing maid, mad at the doctor
who accused him of being God,
playing bank clerk at his window,
pinstripes of rain streaking his pajamas
where his reflection straightens
its waistcoat. Banknotes rip
like bedlinen in the tide of wind.
Down stone stairs tumbles the realm's coinage

heavy with heads. What you hear is the kiss
of tires to wet street, easing away,
chalk taunting blackboard with *erase, erase.*
I'm no sidewalk preacher diagramming
states of grace before the audience
that weather's captured in a doorway
melts off, though the clock
would have it thus. Next week—
why, flying upwards toward the sun,
we freeze.

Sex and Herodotus

Say the Persians were right they saw
no abduction, such women going
willingly or not at all; still, it comes

to provinces plundered for metals
to be coined in a conqueror's likeness—
the etched profile that he, for all

his lording it still mortal, couldn't capture.
Flung, the bronze mirror arced
a dark moon down. Vain as a slavegirl

plumped on the greed that is survival,
a son inherited a war. The historian lied,
as he had learned, about the boundary

blurred between want and need.
To torch crops, not houses, or
the other way around, is to go down

as one who, against a blood sky,
prefigured statues twice his height
shouldering the blaze of memory

against unblistered blue. Barrows
of facts no longer useful were trundled
to the site of the Acropolis and dumped,

more fill on the loll of marble heads,
the chiseled limbs askew. Striking
knucklebones, the ivory dice of famine,

the spade rings, dully. The window
of the Parthenon Restaurant reflects
on temples of bank and burger joint

through which honey's preserved light
drips from racked sweets
where they've been sliced and smears

the knife cutting across a man's stony hand
where it pushes at the small
of a woman's back to hustle her inside.

Pastorale

Praised be the hatching heat
the beautiful boulders under the bridge
the shit of children with its green flies
a sea boiling and no end to it
—ODYSSEUS ELYTIS

Love's anger drives you to speech, to curse
the two-lane road twisting its curves
so tightly you have to slow, taunted

by the stream it parallels. Braiding
like conversation, the creek veneers the digs
of patience hollowing a tumble of rocks,

leaving even in dry season polysyllabics,
so many synonyms for pure force,
passion's simplifications. Water insinuates;

banks erode until pines lean a roof
over streambed and then bridge it in collapse.
You curse that, too, and closeness,

molecules' reckless cascade; and perseverance,
mountain ferried grain by grain
to a distant delta where a farmer skims

blood-brown pine needles off an irrigation ditch.
Up here, in boulder's lee, a water strider
darts toward no safety, no scratch

in the surface's well-argued tension.
You curse the swim of oak leaves, light rafts
quickly swamped. And, crumpled into the slope,

a car body violently, pastorally rusting
into some animal's shelter, then alluvium.

Natural History

Blue as the scattering of particles
that is night sky or deep water,
the whale fins the museum's aquarial light.

Over footstool-sized vertebrae,
engraved whalers crest pink waves,
dwarfed by the hundred pleats

of a throat. Here on sea floor,
its land-bound ancestors rear,
imagined from a few fossils

down to tear ducts their descendants
have no use for. Human skeleton,
whale effigy—with them the Nootka

induce the dead to call it back to shore,
where insupportable cause collapses
under air's clear burden of proof.

Huge lungs flutter shut
in the carnivorous air—oil enough
to burn the tribe's long nights.

Men swarm the beach like sand fleas,
closer to sand than to the enormity
before them, beginning its rot.

Queen of a Small Country

FOR MY MOTHER

1

Even driven horizontal by seething wind,
perpendicular to all notions of gravity,
snow keeps its furious silence
until streets are raged into stillness.
What can we speak of civilly
in the air drowning our footsteps?
Family of imbalances—is love uncalled for
squandered or to be returned? Do we turn
more direct, efficient as a fish-cleaner's knife
sliding along bones? On the river a single
ice-fisherman hugs himself in vigil:
under crust that, unprotesting, bears us
courses something like a submerged anger,
surviving this season one air pocket to the next.

2

Nights that summer of swing shift,
sycamores gloved street lights,
spectral as fingers held over a flashlight,

skin infused red around twigs of bone—
inside the body more opaque than night where,
however cloaked, some presence could always

be discerned—just a black dog
sniffing garbage cans. Arms night-pale
in the available light, breath tearing

in exuberant rags, I pedaled
past moth-swarmed porch lights, televisions'
ghostly gleam, houses vigilant in repose

where a motherly sentry on a prickly couch
drowsed. Or a wife lay alert
for a husband's slackened breathing

that would give her back to herself
a moment before sleep took her as well.
None of these lives was mine.

3

Things we don't have names for acquire them, like couplings,
hardware's "male" and "female" parts, those metaphors part
precise, part lewd, that leave us with the consolation of nam-
ing—my mother winding home by threads of memorized street
names, from those of dead army engineers to those of trees
which in that town were mostly memory, too.

4

A noon whistle rips air to dust,
its motes and beams giving substance
to acute winter light as that mud vessel,
the body, does. How little resemblance
our bodies bear our selves—
Pavlova insisting photos of herself
be retouched, the feet narrowed
to the lithographed points of Taglioni.
Something in me you term beautiful
that, lacking your definition,

I can't see. At the limit
of sighted thought, longing's embodied
by images as much as by lovers.

Queen of a small country unplundered
by school's geography lessons,
she inherited a land like the town
I grew in, plantain and clover
plaited into crowns the short season
before they dried, as if the present
were already being told in another person,
first in the simple past tense, as now,
and soon in the perfect. Like a body
of water, a swirled & floats between us.

Melon Rind, Brain Coral

Pressing the blossom end of a runty,
out-of-season cantaloupe, I trace

the loose knit of a baby's skull,
more cartilaginous fish

than lumbering mammal. What
does the sharp intake of breath promise?

Lungs, those water wings, fill,
buoyancy a physical joy inflated

with a loss unspeakable before memory.
A lone scull of sleep floats those waters

oar by oarstroke, exoskeletal water bug
rippling, ripping sky's reflected cloth

into wakefulness. Vine or reef—
what does the involuntary crash

and tug of breath's waves deliver?
The knit of bone and bone

into a chalky shoal realized skeleton
by skeleton. Over this a finch

marked like no other
flies, flag of the mainland forgotten.

Magnetic Fields

Against waves' *crescendo, decrescendo*
of shore's voices, the rowboat pitches,

cottage roofs bobbing bottled messages
as they diminish. Gulls pennant fog's dim tent

where a cormorant dries oilless wings,
meek, fake mermaid in a sideshow

of disappointment. Once your eyes adjust,
not even appearances deceive; sheer want

is what takes you in, how much you desire
the passion you ascribe a tattooed contortionist,

muscled spray of impossible blue roses
crossing over love's sinewed anchor,

under might's distorted double eagle
with the fluid twine of waves, knots

a net mender knows can't hold. Shuttles
of sound, downstroke and down, a cadenza

of solid chords resists your clumsy pull
on the oars, turned tide tugging you,

kelp-wreathed jetsam, to littoral's wrack
and the high-water mark of cottages'

nautical curtains. The needle
of cramped quarters' small compass quivers

bluely, brokenly, homing to some uncharted pole.

The Garden of Acclimatization

FOR MY FATHER

1

Blanket or sky, at bedtime he leaned
in the doorway blocking all but an aura
of hallway light. I took up the story

from my sister, stalling sleep and his leaving us
in a forest of furniture strange with dark.
To command anything—I steered the tall ship

she'd conjured away from what we couldn't have,
the chink of ice in glasses,
port's lit living rooms, voices lapping late

against each other in tones not lavished on us,
for seas open spills of ink, subtle
with phosphorescence outlining the ship

where it wrote in white the real story:
paper hat given one more fold
to make a boat, its flimsy prow split

the speeding toward a harbor
not curved of his large hands
from the plunge into water's cold welcome.

How water took paper roughly as its own,
not fobbing it off with good-night kisses
as just a story to be dragged under.

2

Scissoring water strider, backwards before me my father
skated, my numb hands caught in his smooth gloves. *Let's
go*, he urged, *let go of me*, and I was rock skimming toward
a drop, kissed and stung by no cruelty but cold. That un-
shattered pane of ice this torn skin, anger smarting at being
unhurt, unwarned. That branch I ducked, spar swinging to
cuff or bolster, my father bending over me, demonstrative as
the blanket, the blank sky.

On a conducting tour, Mendelssohn was approached by a
minor official, once a composer himself, who asked if the
orchestra could play something by his father. Mendelssohn
asked his name. "Mozart," the official replied.

3

Leaves of ice broaden on the lily pond
until a dog can run a tufted duck across it.
Wind's shakedown rattles the beds

and sour kumquats surrendered
scatter from trees splayed against the wall
for warmth. Brought halfway north,

crossed strain with resistant strain,
they toughen under winter's linens.
Accident or design, they pass on

no secret so, brushing it clean,
the gardener rebinds the wound of a graft.
Palms heavy with snow-bloom bend

to be beaten loose with brooms.
Where ground heaved at hard frost
a cheeky cherub grubs, obeisant,

the cut of dirt with three good fingers.
Weathered and parental, the plump
limestone body eaten with age.

Of

Bellflower spilling a candlesnuffer's dark hints—
in such a pooled blue, moon sidles to branch

through a high pane shoved sharply
against sharpened sky. So what we would close in on

recedes: a glossy centerfold dissolves
into modesty—black, cyan sequestered

under magenta's blush, and yellow
unmixing the muddied glow of shaven thigh.

Or, closer, fiddleheads of fern bow
and scrape an air anguished with the O

of lips forced into a blood-flecked kiss,
the sprung trap that hugs a fox's dragging foot.

Short leash, this is how *of* works,
tricked out as *if* in *wife* and the howl in *wolf*.

Circlet of clawed furs collaring a jacket
of skin, glass-eyed, each pelt clamps a tail

hard in the false teeth of possession.
"Make me," the girl in her mother's coat taunts

from a doorway. "You can't make me."
There are limits to what we'll do to each other

on the strength of love or any other weakness;
there must be.

II

And

No longer conjunction lashing
headland's cairn to ocean's winding sheet,

the tide in retreat strips bare strata,
age crushed to age. Wade the slick

of seaweed and soon be islanded
where last century a steamer ran aground.

Three days above heavy seas
helpless mainlanders heard timbers

tear their joins to be tree again.
Water's arms held under, then delivered

the bodies to shore, waters of birth
taking back breath.
                    Ampersand

pink as dead shrimp, the unborn curls
in its tide pool—seed pearl

whose mother lusters over irritant love
it's too late to dislodge;

little anemone, shrinking from touch.
So *and* holds separate what it most closely

binds.

Dream Lectures

1

DOORMAN ON PROPERTIES OF CLOSURE

As you, dear reader, would have been,
in the time of servants,
cinching a lady into her stays,
tugging too hard as she hugged a bedpost—
with the same eager ambivalence, grasp
that a poem might seem to lay itself down
for you to peel veils and husks
of outer- and underwear, heartless
as an onion. Hooks and eyes crowding
at plackets—how the metal tongue
waggles out of the last hole, cocky,
revelation failing such ardor,
your eyes smarting at their own sweet,
diligent closing. The milky stone
of the floor beckons softly, a promise
of rude awakening in the small hours
of a grand hotel where, under your cooled cheek,
the pulse of something rumbles to a halt:
in the darkened palm court a cellist
draws a final bow across the instrument
hugged like a woman between his knees;
and a lily clenches. On a rolled lawn
of green baize, face cards are shuffled
back in with the common ones
while the safe's tumblers rasp and whirl
at the night's take. Where are you
in all this? Down, out with the rest
of the clientele, the privileged

assuming positions indifferent
to any workings but eye-masked sleep.
Deeper, where it is tomorrow already,
a baker strokes a breast of dough.

2

O, wastes and commons of England,
harbors of wild flowers
where barge-like cows munched a measured progress
toward a fair sailing pennants from its masts,
children whirling in pre-Copernican eddies
off to the side of lords who cruised past islands
of animals for sale and men for hire—
lords who swooped, *cormerauntes*,
gredye gulles, over small holdings,
leases swallowed like fish,
who laid out hedgerows and ditches,
though not with their own hands,
which raised the dainty flags
of scented handkerchiefs to thin noses—

it is for you, my sheep,
they engrossed leaseholds, emparked
and enclosed public lands, turning tillage
to sheep-run, that from Down, Oxford,
and Oxford Down breeds would come wool
for the gowns of scholars, not just meat
for the high table but judge's wig as well;
unstinting praise of the larger demesne,
of an economy turned by a queen's decree
that wool make her subjects' hose, cloaks
and shrouds; findings in favor of a future
expert in droppings and the disappearing
Midlands village of the Middle Ages,
for a historian who lauds agrarian reform
as he fingers the rough tweed of his jacket,
a close-cropped weave that reads
the same the wrong side as the right.

What is all this to us? Masters
of taking sides slyly by slow force,
we divide pasture simply
into what's been grazed to the nub
and what remains to be devoured,
up to the church made sheephouse,
gravestones to rub thick backs against.

3
COLERIDGE'S CLOUD

Ere yet the enter'd cloud foreclosed my sight.

That what we contract benignly as disease,
we foster lump by lump sum.
That such attachments as we enter into
pool around us, liquid with assets.
That word be made good
if not as gold, as unriddled wood.
Or else that tenant be enjoined from entry,
squatter as well: rat and field mouse
invading pantry, pigeons billing
in attic filth, ant hauling the half-eaten harp
of a moth wing down a banister.
That, boarded up, windows be blinded
to the stripping room by room
of what, under auction's hammer,
will be knocked down: canopied bed,
rolled carpets' limp tree trunks,
forest floor cleared.
After the right to remain
go the remains, carved into jaunty,
ill-sorted lots and built on by oratory
keen of formula as the trim
on tract houses. What for a ladderback chair
and place settings for three—
for chair, china, and drapes
with a dolorous, pound-sterling air?
Under the expedient hammer comes a window,
a window and the boards pounded over it.
And a slit of light slashed through them,
scarring a blotch of bright wallpaper
where a scene hung, inviting
as only somewhere else can be,
to darken into a varnished night,

going once, going twice. Rights
to the word *was*, finding no takers,
are offered up coupled with *not*.
Pots used to rattling your hooks
as a back door slammed, hat snagged by wind,
how much for the apostrophe of possession?

Passage Overland

So we are saved from death for one another.

The 2 on my ticket is no swan. Dragging
its black train to a rusty siding,
it longs to be 5—southern hemisphere
ripe as mango, a moon down under.

Tall ship, 5 casts off its green seas,
rears into nimbus, no wind coursing the pasture
where cattle lie becalmed, ballast
heaved overboard. Across my reflection,

battlefields blooming with crosses
and villages that tend them waver
under pale masts of a cathedral,
utterly remote, sunk in their museum of air.

So we, at our windows, must seem
to the man pruning a graveyard hedge.
A little death in his shears,
in talon and web. Buried by the spirit,

desires of the flesh rot; mind maddens,
chained in a dark hold; sail turns shroud—
the painter knew. As if to insure
the child Jesus safe flight into Egypt,

he painted the family passing first
through the seventeenth century, his own—
rosy-bricked, plague-ridden Antwerp
blessing them on their way.

So we are saved from one death for another.

Two Rodin Torsos

The Prayer, bronze, 49 1/4″ high
Grand Torso of a Man, bronze, 40″ high

Knee-deep in falling light, she wades
a scuffed surf of sycamore leaves
upstream toward more blinding darks,
already as unseeing as mystics enraptured
envisioning hybrids of torture, each more refined,
more squalid than the last. Arms uplifted
until inflamed, head elsewhere,
thoughtless as prayer from memory—
if she's obeisant in a grove of candles
and reliquaries' fingerbones, she is no penitent
come on her knees miles over gravel and glass.
Promising visitation to the dozen scattered hands
of a saint, she's no supplicant but some man's
calling this body out of clay into bronze:
the calipered breasts, a vague triangled juncture
below the waist between twin monuments of thighs—
pure skin the sculptor's male secretary claimed
an end in itself. Snow in which a mouth
could be gouged. Or so the secretary writes
his wife, making a woman from the street
wait the meal he owes her.

This way, kneeling on the bed, she leans
her forehead against window's cool overlooking
of sidewalk racket. Where a statue's head
should be, surveying the trade in its miniatures,
a pigeon splatters the green-black chest
with medals, lime-white.
                              This way,
in an alcove's must, he fingers

an unblemished sheet of paper. So a room
is paced off. A clearing wedged between stumps
too massive to be moved, even by tears—
pedestals without statues, planted
in a formal garden, they stand on the rudeness
close quarters demand, discreet, turned
half away. In a room mostly bed,
a sculptor pays a woman enough that she'll
let him run his hands over her roughened feet,
then kiss an eyebrow to trace
the bone's socket beneath. The notes
she snugs under a garter, where they dig
a little in the limp marble of flesh,
after she's counted that all she's due is there.

Habit, Those Yards

    Habit, those yards
of black serge scented by incense and beeswax,
    by vegetables pale
from their root cellar and boiled,

    veils the self.
Night-bride, I would wed some other sphere
    than this scorn
of starlings crowning the power pole

    between rumpled sky
and ragged street. In the laundromat
    window's condensation,
someone has lettered a name now weeping

    and pressed a nose
territorially. Wet, black is giving away
    its combination
of submerged blues and reds—wild blackberries

    overrunning a foundation,
overripe late summer, bled into my hands,
    their last resistance
denying surrender with exaggerated wounds.

    Rose of regret,
rose of desire—in the motions of love,
    the smooth machinery
disengages the mind—winter solstice,

a beveled window
fractures into another order
        profligate rays
out of habit thought whole. Between green and blue,

        between jade and aquamarine,
between any two names, an infinite divisibility
        yawns in this,
the fraction that is the visible.

The Corner of Delicious
and Jonathan Streets

Freud claiming that any relation
of two was really comprised of four
wasn't counting intemperate cold

which even the orchards' propellers
can't dispel. A blue-black
more low temperature than tint,

nightfall wraps a tree with a last scarf
of starlings, no insulation.
The one traffic light winks luridly at us

as it must have at the runaway lovers,
fooling no one by sleeping at first
in separate cities.

Warmth lures as much as love,
or passes for it—summer's faraway country
mocks like an out-of-register postcard,

glossy colors loose of the objects
endowing them with memory's worth,
a leaf-infused green the first abstraction.

You become another, at one remove
in the layered embrace of the freeze
whose hold I can't break. Remember

that print where a Japanese courtesan,
paper parasol shielding her plum-blossom skin,
urged her trailing servants bare-ankled

across snow half paper, half ink? Later,
the story unfolded, after her death,
her disconsolate lover carved a flute

of one of her bones. The foot I mean
to plant firmly skates icily forward
and, if you asked now, I would admit

that not the hand you reach toward me
but some balance beyond it
is what I want as we both go down.

Long Island Real Estate:
Great Neck

First, the lawn. This time of day
the shade that carpets it blue
unrolls to the pool now floating
end-of-season apples—all this
was orchard once—but picture yourselves
ripely bobbing there, too. Their side
of the discreet hedge, neighbors follow suit.
Along summer evenings, you'll hear air
turn water—sprinklers' reliable rain,
play screams of swimmers teasing
the mockingbirds' copied, liquid notes.
We'll sell you a sense of island,
screened porch tacked to converted stables—
the mansion itself has gone to tracts—
from whose upper windows you can make out,
over the billows of trees, a strip of Sound,
not much compared to the turquoise belt
of pools the neighborhood sports
but if the wind is right the foghorn carries,
and fog you'll have paid for—as if through it,
dew beading on his brilliant shoes,
on a silver tray a man would bear
an invitation's white meat—you've read
your Fitzgerald. Girls like hothouse flowers.
Hothouse flowers. Fountains jazzily spilling.
One of champagne. A man burning a check good
for eight hundred thousand dollars, leaving
the room before paper's down to the ash
of fiction someone else cleans up.
An afternoon like this, when a fly weaves
at a window screen, you may think you smell horseflesh
but all of that's converted to this, ready
to be sold, and lucky for all of us.

Full Gutters in Beverly Hills

When Dick knocked she had just dressed and
been watching the rain, thinking of some poem,
and of full gutters in Beverly Hills.
   —*Tender Is the Night*

Praise rain's traffic with the wash of trash.
And how, passing for winter, from sky
the gray of old television, it puckers
with goosebumps blue skins

of swimming pools, turning redundant
sprinklers and the man kneeling
to soap a Mercedes. Praise
its indiscriminate industry, worming

under yachts' hatch covers, a convertible
swamped in a parking lot's pond.
Waiting it out, praise drop by drop
of drink as, in the canyons,

mock haciendas lurch and pitch,
room by room giving to the drugged surge
of mud. However close, that's
elsewhere, evening news, an act

of God to be insured against.
Blond floors above all this,
a denimed demi-god is buying a story
you're selling, all rights.

In the engorged Pacific,
a wet-suited surfer rises, slick
as freeway, no allusion to any other myth,
from the cash-green sea.

Piranesi in L.A.

una veduta ideata

And packing sketches, ink, knife, and quills,
down from his imagined vantage point

wound a man as in one of the rococo carriages
he'd drawn, smoothing frock coat and wig.

Foreshortened, the locked curve of freeway exit
straightens, debouching just short of a headwall

of sea—the way his prints take the specks
straggling in foreground toward vistas

of vanishing—sea into itself; canyon overrun
by morning glory gone wild; orchards turned under,

paved over; your hand pointing
to a cliff-hanging house, crossing it out.

Think of kisses the length of stoplights,
red of the WRONG WAY signs that loom before the lost

who want just to turn back
a page to the well-kept neighborhood

of the known, crisp sunlight not islanding a lawn
into an idea. On a copper plate he'd build,

backwards, *una veduta ideata*, rearranging ruins
into a history pretty or grand enough

to be lived in—or slid into an acid bath.
Beneath an entrance ramp to nothing

but unetched lanes of sky, a skater cuts
between cars through shadow's pilings.

To dodge, to touch—feather breaking air bubbles
so acid can bite, or ribbon of shade tying hands

apart—without irony, on love's lasting,
optimistic as this city where what's built wrong

goes down to earthquake, mudslide, wrecking ball
before age has its chance. Full sleeves tied back,

as he etched with the needle what he remembered,
reversed, he spoke to the plate

the anthology of decay.

The Roman Baths at Chesters

Up from a river polished to armor
by raw light, dew takes the rise
blade by blade

to the baths glassed over with it—
the cold room, the tepid, the scalding,
where recruits scrubbed themselves Roman.

Expatriate in exile treacherous
with cleanliness and good pay,
they wrote home for long underwear

and richer food. From them not
what their emperor grandly meant to leave
but the homely cherry, domesticated rose.

Echoes of their chisels in *basilica*,
aqueduct, auxiliaries who patrolled the wall
legions were assigned to build,

one stone against invasion, the next
against revolt. Past the Tiber,
past gray Alps vaguely north,

a ruler's sweeping gesture mortared
miles of air. It wasn't enough,
three and a half centuries

just fishline skimming stream
before surface gives and line sinks,
no longer its own reflection.

Empire of burr and heather,
citizen sheep and rock.

Grounds

Just ribs, the greenhouse floods
with milky, nurturant air—
chambered nautilus laid open,

child's roar of ocean spiraled
down nursery floor. Forgetfulness
sweeps up broken flower pots,

upended cakes of dirt tipsily celebrating
dry years to come, beetles feasting on abandon—
as if again, beneath palms arranged in choirs,

winter lettuce and voluptuous orchids grow
for the mansion, the mansion that isn't there.
Candles flowering in fingerbowls,

pheasant breast sliced on gold-leafed platter,
creamy napkin blotting reddened lips—
Sister, the math is simple:

in houses of the stories that offered escape
from the childhood we called dull,
we would have been the servants,

the view from our attic room
over the master's fair prospects
a calendar's scene, grander lives built

from engravers' cross-hatched days
the way mortals appear on paper money,
ageless faces just lines

green as the lawns their gardeners rolled,
as the limes they had pleached down the path
to the mausoleum. Its marble glows

the dirty white of bones, of bells
of the bindweed that ropes columns,
beginning its own currency

unchecked by the demands of fiction.

The Rich's Laundry

On clothesline's rigging, linens sail,
backyard's boat teased with a landscape
not worn thin as love by use—country

where ports jewel a coast, beckoning,
and out of childhood's encyclopedia
blue cities wake in constellations of windows;

cathedrals filter a forest's green
onto figures stiffened into sainthood
in a clearing of tombs and altars;

a castle's reddened, depopulated rooms
busily glitter. And down a violet river
to a deeply violet sea, lavender sails

belly, shirts opaque with opportunities.
How much of looking is tinged with a love
of longing or loss? *The Book of Knowledge*

pictured women pounding the rich's laundry
clean for a few coins as picturesque,
fair trade with starched and ironed whites

drawing hardship pay continents from home.
But I saw that corruption of the paternal
only later. And lives books told nothing about,

our own, and the tender of love
or its counterfeit in daily barter.

47

Chekhov in Translation

1
THREE SISTERS IN PULLMAN, WASH.

Knotted and tufted with winter wheat,
the Palouse country unrolls
toward grain elevators holding down horizon,
dreamed ships steady as mirage,
crowded with his idea of civilization—
carpets, sprung carriages, and wit
delivered in Arctic wind.
                   Its sweeping
claims shush the cries of coyotes
driven toward chicken coops under the hunter
taking starry aim.
                Starting in the dark
a Russian family unable to afford a horse
would spend much of Sunday walking to Mass,
the rest walking back, thankful
for the kneeling in between.
                  Wind-borne,
wind-sifted, dirt carpets the floorboards
of the theater where a man late for a duel
assures his fiancée nothing's wrong
that can't be remedied by coffee. A glass
of jam-sweetened tea rusts
under the gels.
              Such small measures,
just snow stacking a house of cards
at stage door, lashing epaulets to fences
and the shoulders of a scarecrow, scout
for no winter army.

Next to nothing in time:
the underaged players turning their cars
from Grand Street for the drape of foothills,
the liquor and quick marriages of Moscow, Idaho.

2

THE MOON IN THE PROVINCES

Yakima, Wash.
July 1969

Over round-the-clock industry
of orchard, log jam, and sawmill,
astronauts stumped a treeless moon.
No sharper than shafts of nightlight,
radio waves cracked with words
one of them had rehearsed for the moment
his footprints sank in television's snow—

in the daunting air of the provinces,
climax to a promenade accompanied
by his coughing, a man would treat a woman
from Moscow to Yalta's flea circus—

men seen in miniature moonwalking:
I trailed their diversion awhile. Bored,
pampered fruit swung in ranks,
polishing hints of citified sideboards
groaning with compotes and trifles,
though dusted the dun of an invalid's cheeks—

of a mannequin slumped over yellowed pages
in the town museum, his sleep the one
that makes up history. How lifelike
his seeming breath, his solitude
whittled to splinters by mine

as I took in desks stacked on desks,
chairs on the ceiling. Did a sleeve
sweep a pen to the floor?

                  I lived alone.
To clerks I spoke my first words some days,
thanks. If what I saw in that basement was just
a guard stealing a nap, then I was perfectly
ordinary, too, unburdened by visions.
Like the playwright's ideal wife, an actress
kept by career in a distant city,
the companionable moon rode overhead
faithfully night after night as if untouched.

3

BLACK SEA

Is every story underpinned by sex
or death? Weigh the black sea
buoying a steamer aimed to miss the dock,
its engines killed, so that the current

will drag it home—just surface drift
over what plumbs deeper: past sea urchins
and brittle stars, past diving bells,
past bottom-feeders rooting in the muck

of the continental shelf, down
where no part of light but blue
strains and it giving out, phosphorescent squid
trail fitful constellations

over abyssal hills and plains. Depth
inky with greater depth, here lies sleep
to submerge in rather than be touched
through nightgown,

through watertight diving dress,
be loosed of weighted breastplate and boots
and claimed by the slick of surface,
hauled into someone's arms like catch

or rescue. Fathoms above mollusks
lolling in the murk, ripe for dalliance,
a man loiters where a lady, too well-dressed
for Death, walks her lapdog along the quay.

4
ICON

Metal laid over all but an icon's hands and face,
silver sheet pounded and buffed into clothes

leaving a Virgin more precious, naked,
more remote—not sickbed but river

wrinkles into that foil, though from here
you can't see more than sky shot through

with its reflection, bright coat of paint
your face in water wears, not pain.

The river's set with tumbleweeds this season
and lengthening nights their filigree fills

with ruby, with topaz flame—
in thorny hands the orb that's earth

spinning in the flicker of votive lights—
next morning's ashes offering no relics

but the silver leaf of ash. The river,
risen its banks, binds up logs of char,

rounding on heat-split rocks, smoothing,
abrading, dry hands to fever, stripping damp linens.

Through these wavering rooms it beds down blankets
of curse or cure, shushing the asking

Where does it hurt? And when you move
or laugh? When you lie still and breathe in?

5

FRESH OYSTERS

Not the consumptive's ragged lungs,
not the crumpled handkerchief staunched
against a red and racking cough—

no, like bonnets and puffed pocket-squares,
shells strewed the beach, strayed
from the midden of grand meals past.

Crinolines, encrusted christening gowns,
they preened for the envy of costumiers,
no hurry for the slow accretions

of their history to be scrawled by doctors
impatient of patients' layered modesties,
raring to pursue pain's taxonomy,

to stitch the shell-holding hands
of novice shuckers slipped into by knives,
nothing to be learned from the women

who shucked for a living: they were too good,
surgeons slitting the gristled hinges,
sea-liquor slopped in one bowl,

meat into another. In the shell
of a shed, slickered and booted,
the women worked back of a restaurant

renowned for its glassed-in overlook
and the platters barging into view
sea-fruits raw on half-shells,

those smashed teacups, pearly depressions
waiting to be salvaged, crushed,
sold to pave drives and rail crossings—

not the St. Petersburg train,
the crates, the beds of ice, the coffin
in the car marked 'Fresh Oysters.'

III

There, There

How many photos did we figure in today,
background by accident to couples
blocking the foreign with their bodies,
documenting license to forget?
All the day's budget I spent on postcards;
blanketing the bed, they spill their mosaic
to the floor, covering all approaches
to what floats out the window unstormed.

Look on with me, with a little forbearance,
judicious as a tourist before something
not living up to pictures, of an author
choosing an exotic locale to kill a character.
Were we *there*? No. A woman sold us,
by means of no common language, salt bread
and bottled water. No. Left on a villa's steps,
the camera corrodes in air thick with ruins.
The eyes in the painting saw us everywhere
as the guidebook promised. And the pensione,
this room, frescoed ceiling scabrous with cloud.

No. In the painting that is this piazza,
nothing moves but subsides, rusty bridge
over algal water drowned as the dress
of the woman who crosses them
until she is gone, not to some ill-lit house,
it doesn't matter, but brushed under
by the hour. These islands
cobbled into a city accede a little more
to the smothering daily demands of sea.

Tristan on Radio

And now, over the swell of sea into storm,
in rigging even more symphonic,
a sailor sings of what curves away—
ship that made a night's companion
gone, moth to lamp lit by a woman
and held aloft, beacon over the shoals
of his body. She turned from him to a window
so black it was blind to anything deeper.
If he was bent on leaving, why wait
till first light?
                    So, scanning the unmoving
ruffle of canvas waves, he sings for a wind
and its woman, curtain rising on a muslin ship
taking the stage, the roll of chords
over an Isolde adrift in her own story,
making the song of a man she knows nothing of
cover herself.
                    From the dress circle,
a gloved hand reaching tiers down
to resubmerge a toy ship—no, farther:
over radio's remote susurration,
a sailor sings the last bars and then
it's the usual matter of love and death
up close. From his end of the deck,
Tristan sights for land where, when a woman
who has healed him raises his own sword
against him, this time he would fail
to stay her hand with all he could muster,
a look fierce with undefended islands.
Two voices braid into upbraiding each other
in words wooded with consonants—
into an announcer's translated promises, frenzied
with revision: *Isolde's own magic;*

or a broader one—say, love; or unhappiness
love-induced; or desire passing for love;
or many other things—backlit backdrop
the ship makes from on a tide of applause.
From the couch where she's languished,
a hefty soprano springs up for curtain calls,
done with the easy part, the dying for love.

Eurydice in Asylum

Doctors donning their white coats,
the statues shrug on a first snow.
To the Eurydice who weaves
between burlap-wrapped bushes,

slippers in hand, the clot of nurses
is all encouragement, holding out a coat
like the possibility of again loving
a man more than these grounds,

arguing that she's no composer
preferring trees to his fellows—
what did that gain him, squinting
at a sheaf of scratched notes,

not hearing the birds silhouetted in quavers?
Random music assaulting the healthy ear—
what he would have done for rain's swill
down slates, the snap of her faded blouse

on the line, dropping its arms
in defeat's upside-down victory.
A broom whispers hoarsely
against a warrior's carved cheekbones

to his immense, unfaltering gaze—
across hedge, down slope, at another statue,
a winged one who, over a stone-feathered shoulder,
looks through him with the coolness

after passion or grief—it doesn't matter which,
minor chord resolving to major,
siren and a radio's faint waves slapping
against the wall where staff on break

catch a little sun. A nurse unpins the crackle
of her blazingly blank coif. Practiced,
another urges Eurydice's arms
into long white sleeves. Down the walk

men work wooden boxes over statues
until they're like sentries or bathers changing,
tracing the untouched outline
of a tree's razed history in the grain of wood.

To Market

Uncrated by thunder, first drops against slate
erase the diagonal light that showered

dry as sanctity on us. In air this close
we're worldly, unsalvageable,

water and salt reminders of tide pools'
unabashed stench. To be other—

saintly as turnips' shaved heads
rolled in a box, scarecrow flapping

at its stake, flaring at endearments
as at blasphemy. "Love," the vendor snarls

over his meaty shoulder, "where's
the bleeding knife?" Tearing the cowl

off a cabbage, he turns on me,
backed by onions' choked ranks: "And what

can I do for you, my love?" Tell me
what you call each other when you mean love

less blade than lure. Down the walk
a man meditates over something he cradles

from the rain—the blank martyred face
of a cauliflower in its nimbus of leaves.

Graces

Mrs. D, Mrs. I, Mrs. FFI,
Mrs. C, Mrs. U, Mrs. LTY
   —*jump-rope rhyme*

Sail of her dress billowing,
wide hat anchored by her thin hand,
a girl scudded toward the racket
of this season's carnival—rickety rides
through a painted, peeling foreign country.
She assailed the wind with no question,
any climate the climate of song,

though a murderous heat walls in the houses,
siege of the dead of summer.
You take books in cheap editions
into your long cold baths. Turned thirty,
I list reasons not to have a child
as if reasons were enough and this day
not like any other. Rusty nail,
broken bottle, falling palm frond
slicing the air like a blade—

what couldn't go wrong? In the old story
a fairy wishes a child the best
it can—a little misfortune.
A psychiatrist hopes for his patient
ordinary unhappiness. In another country
the sense of house arrest would be

all too literal, heavy curtains
keeping out more than weather. In half-light

a woman might unfold a worn letter
telling her nothing but that it arrived
from somewhere else, full of news
good enough to be obliterated
by some zealous censor
on its way to her hands.

Second Movement: Adagio

Goaded by a lover's interrogation
    to speak
what will wound, someone eyes
    a window's midnight:

not a lesson-smudged slate
    but rude reflection,
a blotched face moonlike
    in branches' snare.

The backless mirror doubles the room,
    a tree espaliered
into wallpaper, a floating bed
    their bodies

no longer anchor. Words breath-smudged
    onto glass—
what I did had so little
    to do with you,

was done out of no love
    but for comfort
of the strange. For caresses elegiac
    of nothing before—

hand run along a piano's
    curved planks,
not wood now but instrument.
    Rotten forest

petrified, pressured until it burns
      as peat, coal,
or with the hard ashen glow
      of diamond,

nothing to do with pain.
      Roots undermined,
a tree slashes a pond and reverberates
      into ripples, waves

dividing a piano's strings, blood's
      pulse of hurt,
broken chord brought to surface
      note by note.

Laundry

Nights I learn your body as if blind,
    but only *as if*,
and mornings, touching a lit world,

lose scale of dark's intimate topography.
    Memory's sensuous defiance
robs us of more than each other.

A shiver of trees, stripped even of the frost
    that laced them yesterday—
not a woman stepped from undergarments; starker—

Baroque music played without ornament.
    On the radio the last
variation winds exposed clockwork down,

small monument to history's ironic justice,
    taking the name
not of the count who commissioned

a few gentle and happy pieces
    against sleeplessness
but his harpsichordist. *Dear Goldberg,*

the man would be wakened, *play one of my*
    variations. This morning
I could be that woman next door hauling in

a string of laundry. That stiff shirt
    taking no body's
but the wind's bitter shape. What will

keep of this winter may not be
        what we want, the way
a dotted note sustains a tone—but

just a little and then lets go.

Life Drawing

Through air twined with turpentine
and fixative, a viny light
snakes across the model, cold

on oilcloth in a forest of easels.
She's supposed to be the lumps and hollows
of pure form, the nude in the grove

companioned by two overdressed men
who gaze—past the elegant arch
of her sturdy foot, its formal echo

in finger's crook, cheek, whorled ear,
not to say breast—at flesh tones
of bread and peaches. Without turning

her body from them, she looks away,
amused how what we view too long with love
we stop seeing for the fabric of knowing.

Who can bear to believe her, less sexual
than wild orchid's purpled lips and hood?
The model doesn't acknowledge

the body's discomfort, in goosebumped defiance
proclaiming skin a paper unscarred
by reckless line or reconsidered smudge.

She's already on the sidewalk,
an hour's pay in pocket, buying coffee
so hot it scalds speech. Or home,

letting her blouse be unbuttoned.
I give her this body of knowledge;
and distant smoky hills; and their resinous,

volatile explanations of the haze;
and a grove somewhere that seems empty now,
where parasite depends on host,

predator on prey, fiercely close.

This Underwater Room
Where You Swim, Scaled

Harbor light ripples the walls
until we're submerged in summer's deep air.

Fronds of other voices undulate our own—
gull scoffing a fisherman's seaweed catch,

child crying an eye full of sand,
drowning carping neighbors. In this blued room,

we argue water's color versus light's—
blue mirrors, blank windows, that reversed house

this one must reflect, this blue
not so much present as remembered, imperfectly,

the too-easy blur given loss or love.
I want to be the woman opening the door,

squinting in the hard, even sun—
the Venetian air Canaletto painted

in all his pictures, even those of inclement England,
the one sky he'd learned being enough

or easier. She laughs at something too small
or maybe too large to see from here;

seaweed crackles, drying—just ornament
to ocean's *obbligato*, its steady

motor's song, its voiceless fish.

Precipitation

It comes down, it falls everywhere like some ruined hug
of canyons and wings, solitude and snow.
  —MIGUEL HERNANDEZ

Juncos, trying to feed, land on snow
so airy they have to swim it
with the arrested motions of dream

the way clouds do, in their slow collisions
with hills. This season, land's
under forms of water. The ordinary's

white-sheeted like the cheap
summer furniture it is, angles obscured,
hinting not itself, unfaithful reproduction,

but some sturdier original. A life
where I abandon metaphor
for the obscenities you're fond of

and find them another grammar
of evasion, no closer to bone,
no more accurate about love

and its guises—sex or a couple
of brown winter pears nudging
on the sill, looking overripe

but still green-hard. Or this snowlight
that bares us of shadow. Cutting
into a pear, you draw the knife

back toward your thumb. Dreading
the blade's slippage through skin,
later I will remember, wrongly,

your hand blooming red, as if
what we wait for as good as happens,
and this is the infidelity—

not other lovers but, like the statue's foot
eroded by petitioners, the one lover
kissed into vagueness.

Exposures

FOR MY BROTHER,
ON HIS TWENTY-FIRST BIRTHDAY

1

That it won't shatter

at the first cut, a block of ice
warms three hours; then, with a chainsaw,
the chef roughs in a long curve of neck,

bowed wings that will smooth
to swan cresting linen with caviar
and butter on its back, cutlery furrowed

in its wake. After the saw's whine,
a chisel gouges between feathers,
the way, out of snow, a harrowing wind hollows

a cave of stillness that men stumble into
from a climb turned against them—
a cave of warmth hacked from the cold

besieging outside, raised a degree.
There's a finishing touch that hides mistakes
in a bucket of water's glaze;

this the gloved chef savors,
coolly dousing a swan the morning
a channel carves through a solid river—

a swan swimming to the edge of the ice
to break more passage with its breast,
beak dipping to crack its reflection.

At the window he drains his glass
and rolls it across his forehead,
the room's light keeping from him

anything else but his handiwork, lifelike,
bluish as those who sleep in snow.

     2
In the slippage of light

the restaurant labels intimate, he's
at ten thousand feet, belayed,
laying out an ascent over the lip
of a coffee cup that's as safe,

he claims, as crossing a street,
driving home. In light drawing out
the slightest distance, his meat and potatoes
loom, cooling like boulders

a glacier took its time delivering
to lower elevations. A mile and a half up,
crag and precipice jut against the heady,
rarefied air of that altitude,

where breath drawn to blow out candles
circling a summit would not be full enough.
Candles mired in icing, men strung together
working to right themselves—he ropes us

into this with what he's asked for:
avalanche probes and shovel, wine
from the toast to his majority splashing
redly down the snowfield of his shirt.

3

Of its own weight

the glacier at the valley's lip cracks,
smiling into a crevasse, purchase

of the mountain's snow to its slopes
precarious as a low-cut bodice to breasts,

high powdered wig to any
but the gravest court's curtsy and pavane.

No mountain but a melting away,
a lady's retreat to her own chambers

where, sweeping low to a lady-in-waiting
as to a king, she's undone.

In a flame-lit mirror, her hair fever-short,
arm welted where blood-let

and, under a black moon's beauty patch,
her cheek pocked—one survival

bares no promise of another.
Though we would ignore the mountain

shifting its enthroned bulk,
monarch meting out a petty justice—

though we'd skirt notice of its panniers
hiked above the trim of treeline,

it grants no way around, each paned view
crowded with centuries stripped away,

tocsin and tumbrel over the tumble of limbs,
bent twigs of two climbers who,

a short while ago, were about to turn back.

To Speak of Water Music

To speak of water musically smoothing
stones as it bends past marsh iris,

temple bell in fog under Mt. Fuji,
is to make too much of the wind chime.

Closer to say curtain of rain
at broken window, to pitch glass notes

against the damp-warped piano. Over our bed
the ceiling maps with waterways a country

like this one where pale rhizomes
generate root by undermining root;

where moss, propagating by division,
lushly furs over having and abandon alike.

Where nothing's required of us but neglect,
closer to say chimney, blocked fireplace,

flues—what surrounds a closeness
not touch, not intimate, whispering

into the ear's shell: evening's
land-sea breeze rowing through forest

over us, drifting spores offshore.
Waves of passage, passion's wash—

only will binds us to anything,
love that is will. Nothing requires us:

this to come back to as if it were home.

Princeton Series of Contemporary Poets

Library of Congress Cataloging-in-Publication Data

Greger, Debora, 1949-
    And.

    (Princeton series of contemporary poets)
    I. Title. II. Series
PS3557.R42A83 1985   811'.54   85-42670
ISBN 0-691-06646-9 (alk. paper)
ISBN 0-691-01423-X (pbk.)